NATIONAL GEOGRAPHIC

W9-BQT-496

Melting Away

PIONEER EDITION

By Glen Phelan

CONTENTS

Melting Aı

Earth's temperature is rising. That is causing weather to change. It is also affecting wildlife.

By Glen Phelan

ay

Glacier National Park is in Montana. It is a beautiful park. It has towering cliffs. It has sharp ridges. It has deep valleys. All of these were made by ice.

Long ago, ice began to carve the rocks. Small pieces of ice could not do all that. But giant ice sheets could. They shaped the park's land.

Ice at Work

How do ice sheets form? Each winter, snow falls. Some of the snow melts in summer. But some stays. Year after year, this snow piles up. The mounds of snow get heavy. This makes the bottom layers of the mounds turn into ice. Then you have an ice sheet!

When an ice sheet gets heavy enough, it moves downhill. The ice sheet is now called a **glacier.**

Glacier National Park is named for its ice. Glaciers have shaped this land for millions of years. They push away soil. They carve valleys.

Glaciers are powerful. But they don't last forever. If the weather heats up, they melt. This happened thousands of years ago. Today, it is happening again.

© DAVID MUENCH, CORBIS

Warmer Waters. *Melting snow and ice formed this lake in Glacier National Park.*

I'm Melting

Many of the park's 26 glaciers are melting away. Take Grinnell Glacier. In 1910, it covered almost 440 acres of land. By 1931, it had shrunk to 290 acres. In 1998, it was only 180 acres. At this rate, Grinnell Glacier could soon melt away. So could the park's other glaciers.

Turning Up the Heat

Why is Grinnell Glacier melting? The park is heating up. It is about 3°F warmer than it was in 1910.

The rest of Earth is warming up too. This is called **global warming.** Since 1850, Earth has warmed about 1°F. Some places have warmed up more. Some have warmed up less.

Worldwide Warming

One degree may seem small. But it is causing big changes. It causes sea ice to melt. This is making life hard for animals that need the ice.

Global warming causes other problems too. For example, oceans are getting warmer. Some animals cannot survive in the warmer water.

The Meltdown

People do not know all the causes of global warming. But one thing is certain. Earth is warming up.

If this goes on, the whole planet could change. Lots of ice could melt. Rivers and oceans could rise and cause floods. Some plants and animals could become **extinct.** That means they could die out forever.

Glacier National Park would change too. Its glaciers would melt away. The park's plants and animals would be in trouble. Some would have to find new homes. Others could die out. Global warming could change life on every part of our planet.

 How is global warming changing the planet?

Snack Food. *A bear cub munches on springtime berries in a meadow in Glacier National Park.*

Causes for Warming

Why is Earth heating up? No one knows for sure. Some scientists blame **carbon dioxide.** That is a gas in the air. It traps heat. There is a lot of carbon dioxide in the air today. That might be why Earth is warmer.

Other scientists blame the sun. The sun's temperature can change. Some scientists think the sun is getting warmer. It may be sending more heat to Earth. This could be one reason why Earth is heating up.

Wordwise

carbon dioxide: a gas in the air that traps heat

extinct: completely gone

glacier: ice that covers land and moves slowly downhill

global warming: worldwide rise in temperature

Arctic Sea Ice Coverage

Rising temperatures have affected the huge sheets of ice surrounding the North Pole. These images show how.

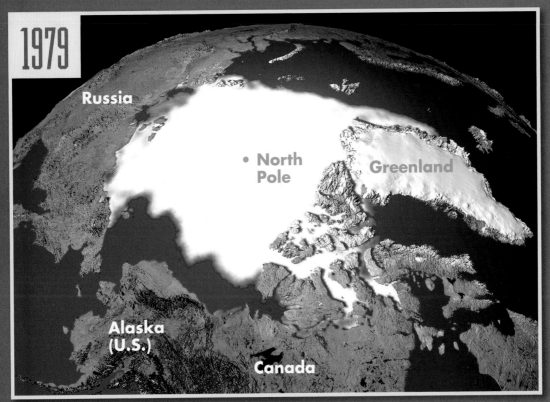

1979

Russia

• North Pole

Greenland

Alaska (U.S.)

Canada

In 1979, ice covered much of the Arctic throughout the year.

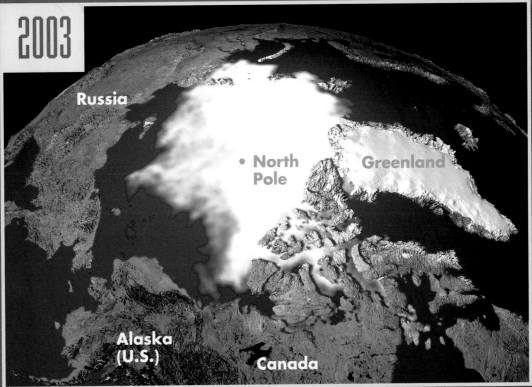

2003

Russia

• North Pole

Greenland

Alaska (U.S.)

Canada

By 2003, large amounts of ice had melted. Where there was once solid ice, there is now ocean water. Many scientists say the ice in the area will continue to melt.

Global Warnings

Most scientists say Earth is heating up. That means changes all over the world. This map shows you what is happening.

JIM WARK, INDEX STOCK IMAGERY

NORTH AMERICA

★ Hudson Bay

★ Utah

NORTH ATLANTIC OCEAN

★ Virgin Islands

SOUTH AMERICA

SOUTH ATLANTIC OCEAN

SOUTH PACIFIC OCEAN

★ Argentina

★ **Utah** Western states have been very dry. As a result, Lake Powell has much less water than usual.

KEVINSCHAFER.COM

★ **Virgin Islands** Warmer weather is causing problems for sea turtles. Many more females are hatching than males. Scientists don't know how that will affect sea turtle populations.

Antarctic Peninsula ★

★ **Argentina** Rising temperatures and water shortages have sparked massive wildfires in recent years.

AP/WIDE WORLD PHOTOS

© KEVIN SCHAFER, CORBIS

© MORALES, AGE FOTOSTOCK AMER

★ **Hudson Bay** Winter ice melts two to three weeks earlier than before. That makes it harder for polar bears to find food.

★ **Bangladesh** In 1998, rain flooded more than half the country. In 2003, floods drove 2.5 million people from their homes.

ARCTIC OCEAN

EUROPE

ASIA

AFRICA

★ Bangladesh

★ Kenya and Tanzania

INDIAN OCEAN

NORTH PACIFIC OCEAN

★ Great Barrier Reef

AUSTRALIA

ANTARCTICA

NG MAPS

★ **Kenya and Tanzania** Malaria, a deadly disease, is spreading. It's carried by mosquitoes. And they love warmer weather.

★ **Antarctic Peninsula**
Winter temperatures are nine degrees higher than in 1950. Sea ice has shrunk by a fifth. These changes make it much tougher for Adélie penguins to survive. Bird populations are sinking.

★ **Great Barrier Reef** Ocean water is slowly growing warmer. The heat is hurting and even killing big pieces of the world's largest coral reef.

Warming Up

Many scientists think people are speeding up global warming. How?

Trashing the Land

People dump tons of trash in the ground. Over time, the trash makes methane gas. Methane traps heat. So Earth gets warmer.

Chopping Down Trees

People also cut down a lot of trees. This is a problem. Trees use carbon dioxide gas. When we cut down trees, more carbon dioxide stays in the air. Carbon dioxide traps heat.

Driving Up Temperatures

People also drive cars. We heat homes. We run factories. All these things put carbon dioxide in the air. This is making Earth warmer.

Making Changes

People may be warming Earth. But we can change our ways. Together, we can help slow the warming. Look at the chart on page 11. What can you do to help slow global warming?

Ways to Slow the Warming

Reduce, reuse, recycle. You can help slow global warming by recycling newspapers, cardboard, glass, and metal. More recycling means that less energy is used to make products.

Spend less time in the car. Your family can give the car a day off. Instead of driving, you can take a bus, ride a bike, or share a ride with someone else.

Buy products that use less energy. For example, some lightbulbs use less electricity than others. Some last longer than others too. Buy only energy–saving products.

Plant trees. Trees use carbon dioxide to make their own food. So planting more trees could help slow global warming. More trees could lead to less carbon dioxide in the air.

Teach others. Share what you know about global warming. Tell other people about ways to save energy and reduce trash. Together you can make an even bigger difference.

Global Warming

Answer the questions to see what you learned about this hot topic.

1 What causes ice sheets to form?

2 How can glaciers change land?

3 Why is Grinnell Glacier melting away?

4 How might people be speeding up global warming?

5 How can people help slow global warming?